CREATIVE COLO

T0089551

Feel good

GALLERY BOOKS

New York London Toronto Sydney New Delhi

Gallery Books
An Imprint of Simon & Schuster, Inc.
1230 Avenue of the Americas
New York, NY 10020

Copyright © 2015 by De Lantaarn b.v., Ede
Originally published in the Netherlands in 2015 by De Lantaarn Publishers
Published by arrangement with De Lantaarn Publishers

All rights reserved, including the right to reproduce this book or portions thereof in any form whatsoever. For information address Gallery Books Subsidiary Rights Department, 1230 Avenue of the Americas, New York, NY 10020

First Gallery Books trade paperback edition January 2017

GALLERY BOOKS and colophon are registered trademarks of Simon & Schuster, Inc.

For information about special discounts for bulk purchases, please contact Simon & Schuster Special Sales at 1-866-506-1949 or business@simonandschuster.com

The Simon & Schuster Speakers Bureau can bring authors to your live event.
For more information or to book an event contact the Simon & Schuster Speakers Bureau at 1-866-248-3049 or visit our website at www.simonspeakers.com.

Manufactured in the United States of America

10 9 8 7 6 5 4 3 2

ISBN 978-1-5011-6232-9

INTRODUCTION

There's nothing like that "feel good moment," when life just seems right and things are going well. In this beautiful book you will find lots of slogans, phrases, and motivational sayings that are surrounded by pretty patterns for you to color in and think about. Select a pattern or a saying that appeals to you, pick up your pencils or pens, and start coloring. Whatever your mood or state of mind, you will find that the relaxation brought on by this simple act will leave you feeling restored, refreshed, inspired—feeling good! For hours of coloring fun and relaxation, all you really need is this book and a little time to sit down and indulge yourself.

ALL you
need
is
Love

From

.....

To

.....

yesterday
is history.
Today
is a gift.
TOMORROW
is a
mystery.

From

To

HOME
is
where
the
HEART
is

From

.....

To

.....

Imagination
WILL
BRING
YOU
everywhere

From

.....

To

.....

GO
where
YOUR
dreams
take
you

From

To

WHEN
nothing
GOES
right
go
LEFT

From

.....

To

.....

Be
who YOU
ARE,
not who
YOU want
to be.

From

.....

To

.....

IF
mama
ain't
happy
NOBODY
AIN'T
HAPPY

From

.....

To

.....

IF you
can
dream it
you can
do it

From

.....

To

.....

LIVE
a
LITTLE
Love
a
LOT

From

.....

To

.....

BE
yourself
and NOT
a copy

From

.....

To

.....

A
cup OF
TEA is
LIKE a
hug

From

To

TAKE
every
chance.
Drop
EVERY
fear.

From

.....

To

.....

the
CREATIVE
adult is
the CHILD
who
survived

From

.....

To

.....

If you put your MIND to it, you can DO it

From

To

you
can't stop
the waves
but you
can
learn to
surf

From

.....

To

.....

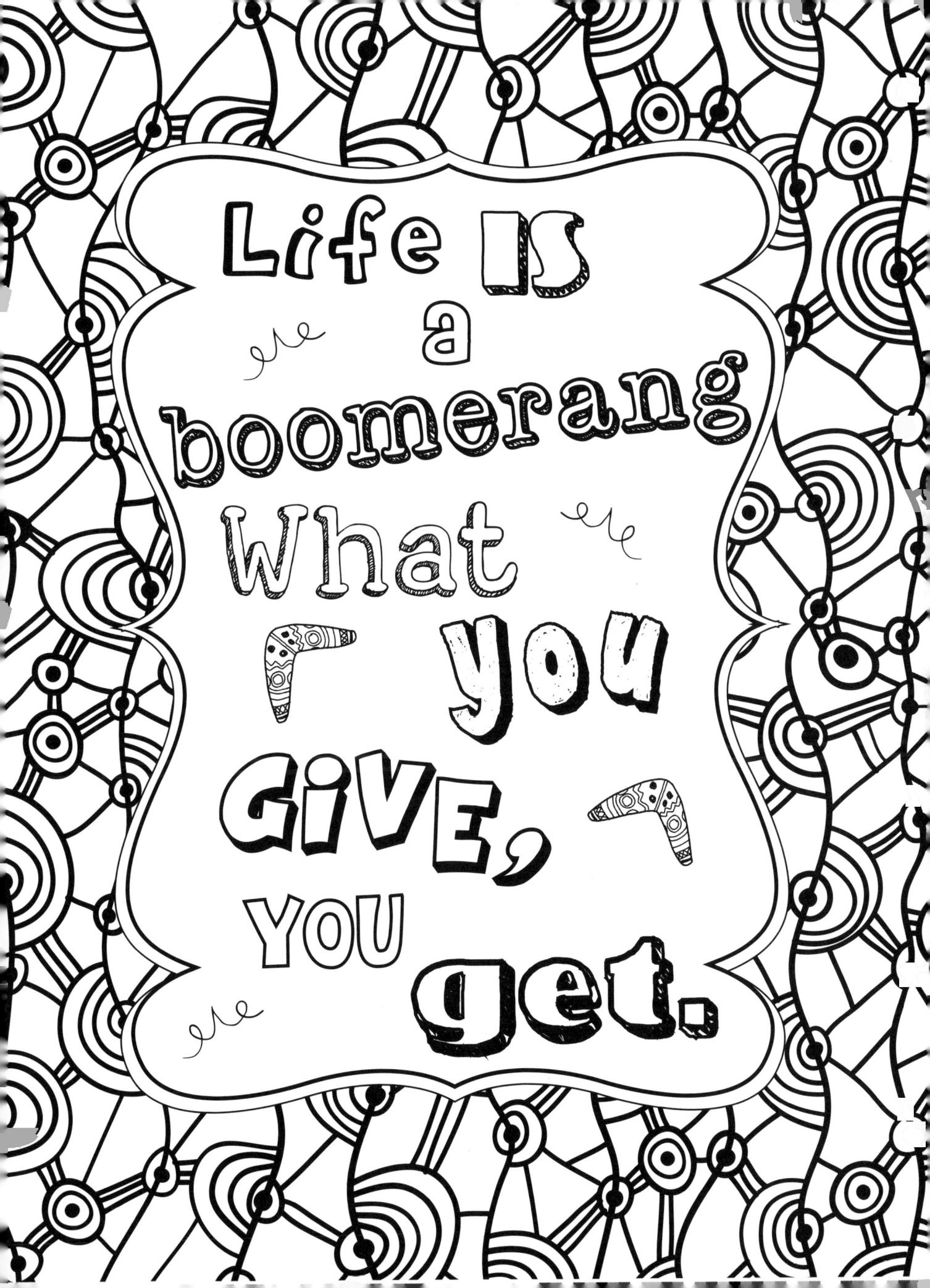
Life is
a
boomerang
What
you
GiVE,
YOU
get.

From

To

Love
builds a
HAPPY
home

From

.....

To

.....

old
WAYS
won't
OPEN
doors

From

.....

To

.....

I
HAVE
a HERO
I call him
DAD

From

To

BE
YOU
tiful!

From

To

every
love
STORY
is
beautiful
but ours
is MY
favorite

From

To

when
THINGS go
wrong
don't GO
with
them.

From

To

if
you
change
nothing,
nothing
will
change

From

To

Live the
life you
LOVE,
love the
life you
live

From

.....

To

.....

ALWAYS
LOOK
on
the
BRIGHT
side of
LIFE

From

.....

To

.....

sometimes
you
WIN
sometimes
YOU
LEARN

From

To

Never
give up
on things
THAT make
YOU
smile

From

To

LOVE
what YOU
DO
DO what
you love

From

.....

To

.....

IT'S
a GOOD
DAY
to have
a good
DAY

From

.....

To

.....

Be the
BEST
VERSION
of
yourself

From

.....

To

.....

Doubt
is the
BEGINNING,
not
THE end,
of wisdom

From

To

DO
more
of WHAT
makes
you
HAPPY

From

.....

To

.....

Live
Laugh
Love

From

.....

To

.....

don't
LOOK back
you're
NOT
GOING
that WAY

From

.....

To

.....

LOVE
yourself
To
love
another

From

To

I
LOVE
YOU to
the
MOON
and
BACK

From

To

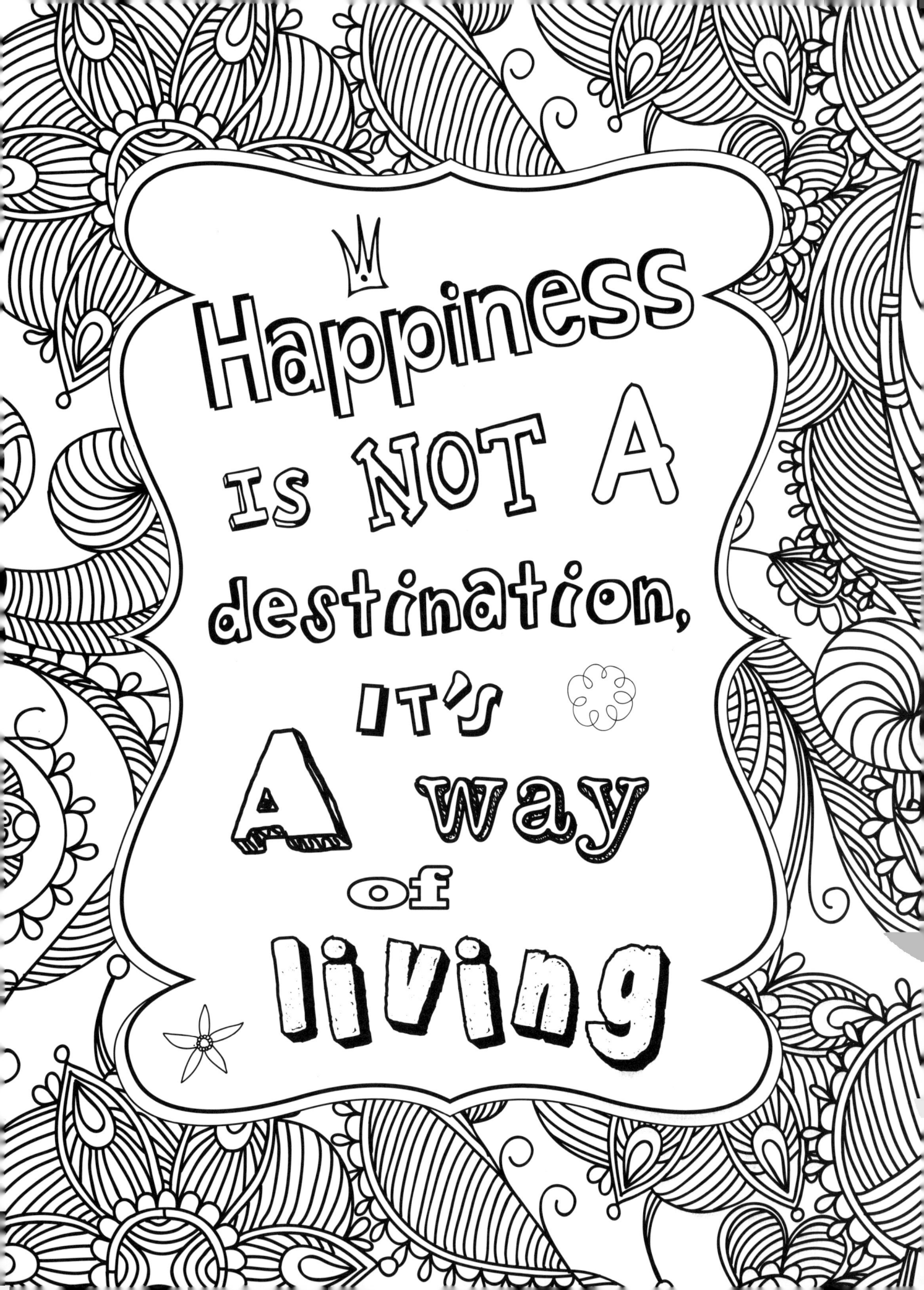
Happiness
Is NOT A
destination,
IT'S
A way
of
living

From

To